T0354629

For This Child
I Prayed

Chloe's Story
A Story of Hope in the Midst of Unbearable Heartache

PENNIE TOMLINSON

WESTBOW
PRESS®
A DIVISION OF THOMAS NELSON
& ZONDERVAN

This book is a work of non-fiction. Unless otherwise noted, the author
and the publisher make no explicit guarantees as to the accuracy of
the information contained in this book and in some cases, names of
people and places have been altered to protect their privacy.

WestBow Press books may be ordered through booksellers or by contacting:

WestBow Press
A Division of Thomas Nelson & Zondervan
1663 Liberty Drive
Bloomington, IN 47403
www.westbowpress.com
1 (866) 928-1240

ISBN: 978-1-9736-2331-1 (sc)
ISBN: 978-1-9736-2332-8 (hc)
ISBN: 978-1-9736-2330-4 (e)

Library of Congress Control Number: 2018903334

Print information available on the last page.

WestBow Press rev. date: 03/22/2018

Contents

Contents

Chloe, age four

Shine Eye

I have prayed for this child, and the Lord has granted me what I asked of Him.

—1 Samuel 1:27

Front Cover Sketch of *Shine Eye*

By j. MacDonald Henry

Used with permission, June 26, 2008

Shine Eye

Artist j. MacDonald Henry
with Pennie Tomlinson

To the young girl in Jamaica who loved this newborn enough to surrender her to another forever family. Life can be very challenging for a single mother anywhere; however, in Jamaica where there is little industry, jobs are hard to find, and it can sometimes be next to impossible to meet the needs of a little one.

This birth mother prayed for her little one to thrive and receive the opportunities of a life raised by a couple who would love, nurture, and provide for her.

God bless you for your sacrificial act of love for this child.

For this child I prayed.

Foreword

In these pages Miss Pennie (as we have come to know and love her) writes of the leading and the following of the Holy Spirit.

She takes us on her journey, tells of her promise, of her granddaughter, and of her daughter, and testifies of the great move of God to unite a photo of a baby with a family who had quite literally prayed the prayers of Hannah.

It is an extraordinary memoir of obedience and the supernatural story of providence. This photo, which was placed in Pennie's hand and on her heart, would become both the beginning of her journey and the amazing evidence of a God that cares about a grandmother's heart, a birth mother's hope, and an adoptive mother's dream.

In these pages Miss Pennie weaves together truth, tears, and triumph. She reminds us in the most eloquent of ways of the faithfulness of God and the fearlessness of a woman led by the Holy Spirit.

She inspires us to remember that God's timing is always perfect, that He is always good, and that we are always forefront on His mind. He is indeed the author of dreams and the finisher of hope.

Pastor J. Brian Hill, worship leader/songwriter

with Cathy Hill, writer/blogger for Clothesline Grace

Acknowledgments

So grateful to Faith Christian Center (Shekinah Revival Ministries) in Holland, Michigan for the excellent teachings, for supporting me on the Mission Field in Jamaica and for their heartfelt prayers.

A sincere thank you to my dear church sister Barb in Michigan who heard from God and orchestrated the time in Ohio

Bless you Grace, the dear saint who travelled from Jamaica to Ohio in obedience that resulted in our divine appointment.

Thank you to the powerful prayer partners in West Michigan, West Virginia, and Jamaica who met regularly for their often gut-wrenching crying out to God on our behalf in Jamaica.

To our dear friend Donna, thank you for your generous help in making flight arrangements and your many prayers.

I am grateful to Bauer Community Fellowship in Hudsonville, Michigan, home church to Michael and Kelle at the time that this amazing story unfolded, for their incredible support, encouragement, and embracement of our little princess.

To my home church and the dear saints of Sanctuary Church in Batavia, Illinois, I am grateful for your tangible love, encouragement, and support in the writing and the publication of *For This Child I Prayed.*

To my friend and fellow sister in ministry Sue Holsinger, thank you for inviting me on a marvelous getaway where I could sort out my thoughts, hear from the heart of God and for introducing me to your friends Tom and Chris.

To Tom and Chris Routh, precious saints instrumental in helping me persist in the challenging effort of writing this story, you offered your beautiful and serene cabin in the woods environment as a retreat for an incredible week, and you contributed significantly to spring boarding this project.

To Pastor J. Brian and Sister Cathy Hill, who have become such dear friends, for your invaluable contribution in counsel, suggestions, and consistent support.

A sincere thank-you goes to Michael and Kelle for their

willingness to share this very private journey of pain, grief, and disappointment. They experienced the faithfulness of God during those earlier days and watched God's perfect plan unfold in His way and in His timing, and they chose to share this journey with you.

Thanks to Michael and Kelle's amazing sisters, Jodi, Kelly, Jill, and Nicole, who walked with them through their heartache of thirteen years of infertility and seemingly unanswered prayers. That support followed them from those early days right to the final step of the journey at the airport to the time they brought their new child home in the middle of the night.

Thanks to j. MacDonald Henry, a dear friend and artist of the original sketch- *Shine Eye;* which is a tangible and major piece of this memoir.

My ultimate thank-you goes to my heavenly Father, who without His loving and watchful care, His guiding Holy Spirit, His patience, and His clear direction; I would not even be able to breathe. Thank You for entrusting me with this amazing assignment. May You alone be glorified.

Introduction

In my heart I had a desire to write down the details of Chloe's beginnings. The more I thought of it, the more intense the urge became. On a Wednesday afternoon, walking from the elevator to my apartment in Michigan, God gave me the title for Chloe's story, *For This Child I Prayed.*

That very evening in a church service, the pastor spoke about a woman named Hannah in the Bible, who is found in 1 Samuel 1. He said that God had closed her womb. She earnestly prayed for years for a child. Then one day, as written in 1 Samuel 1:6, "Hannah was in deep anguish and grief, weeping bitterly and she made a vow to the Lord praying again for a baby. She promised to dedicate her child back to God."

I began to sob. Had God not closed my daughter

Kelle's womb, she and her husband, Michael, would not have pursued the avenue they did.

When I understood how significant this truth was, I knew I needed to put this journey on paper for my granddaughter Chloe. I also believe it will be a true source of encouragement to those dealing with issues that only God can get them through. So began this very exciting and dramatic assignment of sharing our experience.

But I am getting ahead of myself here, so let me start at the beginning, set the scene, and introduce you to the characters that make up this incredible story.

Prologue

This true story will share of heartache, drama, danger, and hope. A teen's dilemma ultimately fulfills the cries in the night of a couple nearly two-thousand miles away.

CHAPTER 1

Framed Treasure
Angel Unaware

How many people does it take to make a difference? It had been my prayer for years that my actions would have a positive and lasting effect on others, and I aimed to do just that.

With a passion for garage sales and antique shops, my dear friend Chris and I set out for a day of exploring to see what treasures we could find. We did things like that most weekends, never knowing where we would end up but always having an adventure. While perusing an antique shop forty-five miles from home, I began digging through a baby bassinet filled with photos. There at the very bottom of the pile, I came across a framed sketch of a precious black child with earrings. The beautiful little girl captured my heart so much that I could not put her down for fear someone else would snatch her up. How could I let go of her? Her huge almond eyes seemed to reach deep into my soul. She looked so innocent and yet had a spark of playfulness. I knew then and there that she would be going home with me. It would be nearly a decade later before I knew the significance of this sketch and this little girl herself, but she always had a place of honor in my home as if I knew her personally.

Early in 1996, my youngest of three daughters married a great Caucasian fellow. I had always sensed I would be surrounded by dark-skinned grandchildren one day; however it didn't appear that would be the case now that my last daughter was married. Little did I know what was about to unfold.

I will never forget the day after Thanksgiving. There was a beautiful CD of piano music playing in the background, the warmth of the sun beaming through the window on a chilly morning, and me comfortably going through my notes from the previous week's Bible school class. We were reviewing the topic of missionaries. Two-thirds into my study time, I heard the words, "You will be moving to Jamaica to do ministry." This was such a tangible voice that I initially thought, *Did someone enter the house without even knocking?* Although I knew better, I still felt a need to look up from my computer to confirm I was indeed alone. I knew in my spirit that God was speaking to me. Then I said, "Jamaica? Are You sure?" After that, I found myself chuckling at the mere thought that God wouldn't be sure.

In just days following what I believed was a revelation about my future, I shared the news with my pastors, elders of the church, friends, and of course, my beloved daughters. I was so excited that I would share the news with anyone who would listen. I made a trip to the library to find all I could about Jamaica (including where it was on the map). My pastor was supportive and said that if I truly felt this was a calling, I should begin to do those things that would help me stay on course. My elders encouraged me to stay with the Bible school for at least another year and advised me on pursuing this call. They lined me up with a couple who were serving in Montego Bay, Jamaica, and who our church was currently financially supporting, and I soon scheduled a trip to visit them and see if they were a fit for me. Within days I applied for my passport and thought about prospective renters for my home. In Bible college we learned that if you go into the mission field, you should not liquidate your largest asset for at least the first two years.

My friends had mixed feelings. While they were excited for me and the prospect, none of them were too ready to let their friend travel thousands of miles away without knowing when she would be back. I believe one of the greatest joys was sharing this vision with my daughters, Jill (twenty-eight), Kelle (twenty-six), and Nicole (twenty-four). They were each happily married, and Jill even had an adorable three-year-old son. These three amazing young women were always my biggest cheerleaders. They knew my heart well and shared in the thrill that God had spoken to me in such a straightforward way and also that He had an amazing plan for my life. We all knew it would not be easy to live apart from one another, but we also all wanted to serve God's will for our lives. We knew His grace would see us through the absence.

Even though I didn't feel a connection with the couple in Montego Bay, the commitment to the country of Jamaica felt stronger than ever. In the spring of 1998, on a quiet Friday night and following a long workweek, I decided to lay low and stay home for the weekend with just music but with no plans and no television. My heart's desire was to hear from the Lord regarding Jamaica. I had no question in my heart that the call I sensed was real, that I truly would be moving to Jamaica to do ministry work. I had started making preparations, but I had reached a point when I was trying to envision just what this meant. In short, I was ready for more direction.

The following morning I turned on my favorite piano CDs and began my weekly cleaning. I love to throw open the windows and get a bucket of wonderful smelling cleaner and go from room to room. As I was dusting the framed sketch of the precious little girl I had purchased years earlier in the antique shop, I found myself talking to her. I tapped on her sweet cheek and asked, "What are you about, little girl?" Immediately, I felt prompted to go to the kitchen for a sharp knife. I sat down at the table and gently cut the matting loose from the back of the frame.

Pennie with mission display

Imagine my absolute surprise when on the back of the sketch were the words "j. MacDonald Henry—Kingston, Jamaica, 1961." There was my answer. I would move to Kingston in Jamaica. From that very moment, there was never another question regarding the location.

Taken aback with emotion, I remember sitting in place and crying, praising, and praying. I had assumed the little girl was from somewhere in the United States, perhaps even from a Southern state. How could I have imagined that her photo, purchased years before, would be used by God to tell me where I'd be moving to in Jamaica?

In the days following, I continued with my schedule of working, going to church, and attending Bible school. I shared this updated and exciting news with everyone I could. I had a map of Jamaica that I frequently looked at and prayed over, and each time my eyes would land on Kingston, my heart would smile.

On Sundays, a friend I called Mury as a term of endearment, who lived forty-five minutes from our church, came home with me after the morning service. We did this from time to time. We would have a nice dinner, chat, nap in the recliners, and then return to the evening service together. She knew all about the marvelous journey regarding Jamaica. In fact, she had accompanied me to Montego Bay the previous year.

It was time to pursue the sketch information. My friend had a good point. If the author of the sketch was thirty to forty years old in 1961, he would likely be sixty to seventy years or even older now. Perhaps it was time to call him and find out what I could about him, the little girl, or Jamaica itself.

I don't know if I had ever previously made an international call. Perhaps that was why I felt awkward. My heart was probably overwhelmed about what could transpire next. I dialed Jamaica information, and holding the sketch close to me, I asked the operator for the phone number of j. MacDonald Henry. In a professional tone, she informed me there was no number available for my requested contact. I surprised myself. I didn't even allow myself to feel disappointed. Without hesitation, I responded, "Miss, I believe God wants me to make this connection. Please do what you can to help".

She put down the phone, and I could hear her talking but not to me. I said to my friend that something weird was going on.

A sweet voice took over the call. I told my friend that I was talking to a different person now. The very pleasant operator said, "Miss, try this number, and have a blessed day." That was awkward, but I simply thanked her and said, "God bless you," and hung up.

When I gathered my senses, I started shaking and asked my friend what had just happened. Was this an angelic intervention? It seemed so. I would have been satisfied with basking in this memory for a day, a week, or more, but my friend prompted me to push through and make the next call to j. MacDonald Henry. I was anxious. I didn't want to run into a dead end or meet with a rejection. Just then faith rose again. I acknowledged the fact that this whole journey had been incredibly unusual. After all, the first operator said the number was not even available.

I dialed the number given to me. I had paper and pencil in front of me in the event I didn't remember the details of the call. I didn't know what to expect, but I knew an incredible event was unfolding in front of me.

"Hello," a woman's voice said. I explained who I was and mentioned I had a sketch in front of me of a little black girl with her hands drawn up to her face. I shared that this little angelic child had captured my heart years ago and that I hoped I would be able to find out about the artist j. MacDonald Henry. I asked if she knew him or any of his family.

She responded, "I am Jeanne MacDonald Henry, the artist." I remember clearly laying my head down on the table in front of me, tears welling in my eyes. How could this be? I then explained that I believed I had been led by the Lord to move to Jamaica to do ministry work.

It felt like we had known each other and that we were longtime friends. She shared that she herself was captured by this same little girl and that she had taken a photo of her and then sketched from the photo. She proceeded to ask me my field of interest and my qualifications. I didn't feel I had anything special to offer and simply told her a little about myself. I stated that I was a Christian, that I took psychology in college, that I was an operator on a suicide-prevention crisis phone line and trained others in the same area, and that I worked as a counselor with Women in Transition, a crisis line for women going through some sort of trauma and/or transition. I added that I was computer literate. She immediately said that she would line up appointments for me in those fields, and she asked when I could be there. *Are you serious?* I thought to myself. This amazing and world-renowned artist was going to assist me in this endeavor? I would graduate from Bible College in June, and I answered her by giving her the day following that date as my flight day.

When we came to the end of the call, she said she would have her driver meet me at the airport. I just needed to give her the flight times and information when I made my reservation. Just before we hung up the phone, she asked me how I had learned her phone number. I told her the story of the two operators and the sequence of events. She chuckled and said, "Oh, because you see, it is unlisted." Somehow, I knew there was divine intervention in my obtaining that number.

Just as Jeanne had said, her driver greeted me at the airport. He drove me and my friend who accompanied me to a Catholic convent where we would stay for the next week. We agreed we would connect in the morning with Jeanne and discuss a plan. She gave me a list of times, dates, and phone numbers for arranged appointments. I remember going up many flights of stairs in a very dark building on Spanish Town Road to apply as a family counselor, walking to the Wortley Home on Constant Spring Road to apply for a housemother job for little girls, and visiting several other places.

One decline letter after another came to me, all stating I was overqualified. *Seriously? I am a volunteer*, I thought. *How can I be overqualified?*

I see now that God closed those doors, waiting for His choice of place and His timing.

CHAPTER 2

Divine Appointment

In the fall of 1997, I continued in Bible school with seemingly no immediate direction. In the spring of the following year, a church sister, Barb, called me and told me the Lord had directed her to take me to Ohio for a weeklong camp meeting. I told her I only had one week of vacation left and felt I needed to keep it in the event I needed to go to Jamaica for an interview. She insisted, and it seemed to me the Lord could use this forum to show me more if He chose to, so I agreed. Life would never be the same.

On the first night of meetings, we were asked to sign a paper that detailed what we were asking God for during this week at the camp meeting. I wrote down that I hoped for specific direction regarding Jamaica and where in Kingston I would be going.

During the day, we would go to meetings, stand in long lines, and wait in the hot sun or rain. Then once we made it inside the building, we would scurry around, looking for the best seats possible. On the final day, there was a meeting for partners of the host ministry. Since I was not a partner, I told my friend I was just going to stay at the hotel to have a quiet day and prepare for the keynote speaker that night. Her response was profound. "You have come this far to hear the voice of God in response to your future, and you are going to skip out on this meeting?" She was right. I quickly got dressed, and off we went to stand in the long lines once again.

When we got to the hectic and chaotic auditorium, we found seats and began to settle in. I felt a prompting to change seats, which seemed a bit ridiculous. People were climbing over pews to get to others, and the seat I felt compelled to move to was not any better. However, we got up and moved. Seriously, it was as if angels were guarding the row to save those seats for us.

Immediately after again settling in, I turned around and said to the lady directly behind me, "Are you from

Jamaica?" She was so taken aback. She threw her arms up and said, "Ya, mon." We proceeded to talk for nearly the whole hour of waiting for the event to begin. I told her I would be moving to Jamaica and how that came about. I asked her about her church and their mission statement. I asked if they had an outreach program and a statement of faith. She appeared frustrated and shared she had cleaned out her purse just before coming to the States and had left that information at home. I asked her to check again; and lo and behold, all three of the items I had specifically asked for were there. Something supernatural was transpiring here. I could feel it all throughout my body.

"Where is your church?" I asked her.

"Kingston," she said. "Where are you going in Jamaica?"

"Kingston," I said. We embraced each other and began to weep. There was a connection that we could not explain. Both of us felt it.

I looked at her outreach brochure and said, "I will be responding to the number-five prayer request," which read, "Looking for someone with a heart for children to head up our ministry at the Children's Place of Safety."

In the hours following this God-orchestrated meeting of two people living thousands of miles from one another, the emcee asked people which countries they represented. He would list off a country, and those from that country would call out and clap. In a room filled with thousands of people, I felt prompted to move directly in front of this precious sister from Jamaica. Following the event, we promised to keep in touch. We took several photos together and reviewed what had transpired and how amazing this was.

When I got back to Michigan following the week of meetings in Ohio, I replayed the events over and over, first to my daughters and then to my friends, and they all shared my joy. I made an appointment with my pastor. I shared the events that took place in detail and with excitement. At the end of our visit, my pastor said, "Too bad we don't know the statement of faith of the church in Kingston and their mission statement and if they have an outreach program." We both shared a look of shock when I told him I had gotten all of those brochures from my new friend, Grace! I had wondered why I asked for those items. Little did I know my home church would ask for just those specifics. No more, no less.

There was one last place to bring up to date. I went back to my place of employment and updated my boss. She was delighted to see the dream I had been talking about for two years begin to unfold. She also assured me that when and if the church wanted me to come down for an interview, she would approve of the time when I needed it and allow me to stay as long as I needed. She knew I had used up my vacation, but she also could see God's hand in this all. She was also excited to play a part of it.

I proceeded to write a letter to the church represented on the outreach brochure Grace had given me, and I sent with the letter a short autobiography, my resume and recommendations from my job and my church. I then waited to see if they wanted me to join their ministry. It seemed like months, but the response came in just a few weeks. Yes, there was some interest, and they said they wanted to meet me and hear my story. This was August 7, 1998. Labor Day was in the following month, and I made the trip to Kingston to meet the very church family Grace was from for an interview. I was beside myself with excitement. Each step was one step closer to the dream I had developed two years previously.

The elder overseeing this opportunity at the church in Jamaica told me that if everyone agreed that this was a good fit, I should raise my support and get my affairs in order in the States. When that was all finished, I could come to join their congregation, get to know their ministry and the culture of Jamaica and I would worship with them for two years, and after that time, they would commission me into ministry. An incredible thing transpired at this meeting. The head elder in charge asked the rest of the elders present if they had ever seen the outreach brochure I referenced as a response to their prayer request. No one had, simply because it had never been printed. The one copy that this dear saint Grace had given to me at the camp meeting was a prototype! Before I even left Jamaica that week of this first meeting, I received a letter from this very church encouraging me to raise my support and get back to Jamaica as soon as possible. I would be commissioned into ministry **upon** arrival rather than have to wait for two years. God had made an immediate opening, and they welcomed me eagerly.

In receiving these confirmations, it became exciting to do all the necessary preparations for the move. I lined up renters for my home. I paid off my debts. I began raising my support, and I began to say my proper goodbyes. It was a bittersweet moment with my family, but I had their blessing. They could see divine intervention unfolding the entire way throughout the process. I would have been delighted to leave within weeks, but God has His own timing. Fortunately, He gave me the grace and patience to move in step with Him.

Two years later and with two suitcases, a passport, and the support of my home church, family, and friends, I boarded a jet to Jamaica. It had been nearly four years since I felt the prompting to do so, and after putting all my affairs in order, I was on my way. I remember being on the jet, looking out the window at the vastness of the skies and the amazing formation of the clouds, and sitting there in awe that the Creator of this magnificent universe had plans for me and had His hand on me throughout the journey.

The most challenging part of making this permanent move to the island of Jamaica, which was 1,800 miles from what I had called home for fifty-two years, was leaving my children and my four beautiful grandchildren. The comfort through this particular part of my journey was the fact that my amazing daughters kept me very much informed about the lives of my grandchildren with photos, stories, and phone calls. What a challenge but delight it was to love from afar.

Living was quite different in a third world country.

Every step was a first for me—the food, the language, and the customs. I was alone in this walk, but it felt so natural. I simply fell into position, learned many new things each day, met the many challenges head-on, and quite enjoyed the amazing experience.

The next five years were filled with working at the Place of Safety, a children's home for the abandoned, neglected, and orphaned. Each day the forty to sixty children would line up, and people would measure them for pants and shirts. They would find their places at the large table, and staff would hand out bowls of whatever was being served all around the table. The little ones would reach in and eat handfuls without speaking any words. Then they were ushered into the bathroom to relieve themselves and brush their teeth. Thus, their days began. I was privileged to work in this home, but I also helped administrate a school in the backyard that the Friends of the Home had started. A building was erected, and we were protected from the elements. I made their curriculum, supplied teaching aids, and monitored development. In short, I was the children's advocate. Those memories and experiences could have filled a dozen books and they will touch my heart for eternity.

Along with the school, I was overseer of the Mother's Day brunches, Christmas functions, and the general interaction between the children's home and the church I represented. There were more than fifty volunteers, who assisted to make for a lovely ambiance, a lovely meal, entertainment, gifts, and plaques awarded to the workers for the recognition they so deserved. All had a delightful time. I was also privileged to help head up Star Child, an annual December function where our church entertained five hundred inner-city children for a day of games, activities, devotions, food, and Christmas gifts. Coordinating the purchase of gifts for five hundred children of various ages, wrapping them, and distributing them was quite an adventure. This took a team of hundreds and the generosity of people as far away as the United States to help with the purchase of what we needed.

When I wasn't at the children's home, I helped in the after-school homework center programs, clothing and food distribution ministry for the inner-city communities, and mentoring programs. Along with helping with the teaching, I was designated as the person in charge of the daily devotion delivered at the beginning of their time at the center. At bedtime I would drop into bed, exhausted, but I always had a sense that I had helped in some way, even in a small way. I had alleviated the incredible workload for the government workers but also nurtured the broken, damaged, and very needy little ones who were there through no fault of their own.

The church I linked with in Jamaica asked me if I would consider being a housemother to three little girls of the church who needed a home. When we took a tour of the home they were considering for this new ministry, I saw on the wall a sketch of *Shine Eye*, the very sketch I had purchased years earlier in the antique shop in Michigan. Because this proposition was parallel with my dream, I could see once again that the Lord was working in and through me.

There I was, a grandmother's age, moving from being quite independent and living alone to being mom to three little Jamaican beauties. While maintaining my normal activities at the Children's Place of Safety, the after-school programs, and other places, I added the responsibilities of parenting, homework, shopping for little ones, and overseeing their spiritual and physical care. I loved it.

Living in Jamaica was an incredible experience. The extremes were drastic, and there was a steady stream of surprises. One could listen to people in the streets singing the words to the world-renowned Jamaican artist Bob Marley.

> Get it together in Jamaica,
>
> Soulful town,
>
> Soulful people,
>
> I see you having fun.
>
> Dancing to the reggae rhythm,
>
> Oh, island in the sun!
>
> Come on and smile,
>
> You're in Jamaica!

One minute, I would be basking in the beauty the island of Jamaica offers and it seems in the very next minute there could be gunfire, sirens, and bustling around to get inside for safety.

The rainbows would splash across the sky with the light rains. The amazing flowers would bloom in every color imaginable, and the heavy branches of trees would be laden down with succulent fruits free for the picking.

In contrast, while walking to the market, I would see signs of poverty and children begging in the middle of traffic so that they could buy something to eat, not to mention the strong smell of the "sacred weed" and urine because of the many people living in the streets.

The church across the street from our home was used on Sunday for services, and during the same week, it was used as a political voting station. On Sunday, the hymns would resound with robust energy; however, days later the entire ground would shake, and we would witness a huge army tank filled with soldiers coming to the same venue to break up the violence that left victims in the streets after gunfire.

While riding public transportation, it seemed I was cautiously watching everyone's move, and I got off the bus quickly. I was always grateful to have reached my destination safely.

It is an eerie feeling to be able to say I became accustomed to this bizarre contrast. Many times I didn't feel safe, but I never gave much thought to it. I didn't know what would take place each day, and while most days did hold an element of drama, at the end of the day, I would just put my tired body to bed, lay my head on the pillow and say a prayer of thanks that all was well with my soul.

It was a Tuesday morning, and like other weekdays, it began rather routinely. In this home for little girls who all needed a place to live because of abuse, neglect, or being orphaned, it began with a Jamaican breakfast of breadfruit, plantain, and other routine Jamaican entrees, and preparing the girls for school, which would be out for the summer in just weeks.

We would discuss what we would be doing that evening and what was expected of each child for the day. I would check over their homework, and I would also say a prayer to send them on their way.

This day changed my life forever.

Off to school the pretty little girls went with their crisp navy and white uniforms, heavy backpacks, and freshly platted hair. There were no school buses, so regardless of the weather, the walk to and from school was a routine part of their day. The classrooms were overcrowded and seriously lacked resources. I was grateful that my friends and supporters in the States understood and frequently would partner with us by sending things that would assist me with helping them achieve their best. I also made myself available to assist in the classrooms and contributed what I could to the teachers.

While there seemed to be much lacking in resources, I give the teachers kudos for all they could do with what they had.

Once the girls were off to begin their day, a young girl who was eight months pregnant and had come to live with me stated she had not felt the baby move for a few hours. I called her doctor, and we were advised to head directly to the hospital.

Let me share how I came to know this young soon-to-be birth mother, whom I will also refer to as Mum. The children of Jamaica have this enduring name for their mothers. I will even introduce you to Chloe. *For this child I prayed.*

CHAPTER 3

Heartbreak to Newfound Hope

In May of 2005 during my daily work at the Place of Safety (primarily a short-term placement for abused, orphaned, and/or neglected children), I met a sweet little baby girl named Raquel. I called my daughter Kelle and her husband, Michael, who lived in Michigan, and told them about her. In their thirteen-year marriage, they'd had no children. They had unsuccessfully exhausted their options with doctors and fertility specialists. The doctors didn't know why they couldn't conceive. Their hearts were broken. They wanted nothing more than to have a child of their own. Perhaps they would consider adoption.

Michael was 100 percent on board with adopting, provided that the child was a blond-haired, blue-eyed boy. As things went along, Kelle and Michael acknowledged together that God might have a totally different plan for them.

They began the lengthy and challenging effort of putting all their paperwork together in the hope that they would be able to adopt this child from the Children's Agency of Jamaica. Kelle eventually traveled to Kingston to represent Michael and herself and to formally apply to adopt Raquel. They began to dream of the day when their childless home would be filled with giggles, activities, and the sound of children.

After seven months of dreaming, their hopes came crashing down. At the last minute on Christmas Eve, the children's agency called my daughter all the way in Michigan, 1,800 miles away, to say that the child they had their hearts set on adopting had been placed with another family in Jamaica. "This is the mandate that a child is placed within the country," they stated. It turned out that a baby is never adopted outside of Jamaica unless it's an infant with special needs or an older child who is physically and or mentally challenged in some way. The likelihood of them getting a healthy baby was very low. They were devastated, and Kelle was inconsolable.

No one can describe the emotions that wrenched the

hearts of our family in the weeks to follow. We went from dreaming, praying, and believing to having empty dreams and broken hearts. Had God not answered our prayers? The disappointment was overwhelming. This couple who was one minute so hopeful in believing they would soon begin their family with a child now stopped dreaming. Their hearts were crushed. We didn't talk about it any further, and they stopped considering the possibility—at least for the time being. They weren't getting pregnant, and now the dream of adopting had collapsed, which only compounded the pain. Four months later the phone rang at my home in Jamaica. It was a church sister. A friend of hers knew a friend who knew a friend with a domestic helper who was pregnant. The birth mother knew she could not keep the child, and she did not know where to turn.

This caller was asked if she knew anyone who might be interested in adopting, and she quickly remembered our family's story from the year before, so she gave me a call. She forwarded me the phone number of the woman, and I immediately called the employer of this domestic helper. When the employer asked me when I could come to meet with them, I wanted to answer, "Right now!"

However, we made the arrangements to meet the following morning. My sleep that night was very limited because I was dreaming, praying, pondering, and hoping.

For this child I prayed.

Because my daughter had previously given me a complete copy of all the paperwork they had in place with the children's agency, I was able to bring it with me to meet this young, pregnant, and likely nervous teen. This packet contained employment history, medical history, financial history, photos, recommendations, and much more.

In the taxi ride to her home, my heart pounded. My palms were wet, and my mind raced. Did we dare hope again? Would we set ourselves up for another disappointment? Should we risk opening our hearts only for them to possibly be broken again?

My peace could only come from above when I went to the door with no idea what I would encounter during this meeting. The employer met me and invited me in. She quickly shared her frustration with this young teen. She knew the pregnancy would mean she would lose her helper at least for a while. However; even in her frustration, the employer was caring and helpful in this situation.

The young girl came down the stairs, carrying a

vacuum cleaner. She didn't look pregnant, but she had been doing what she could to hide it from her employer, who had just found out herself. At that time she was six months along and could no longer disguise the situation with larger clothing.

How serious was she about surrendering her newborn? The couple I was about to introduce her to by way of the packet of information was not Jamaican. How would she feel about this child being raised outside of her country? Was this birth mother healthy? What about the birth father and extended family?

Hide your feelings, Pennie. Stay focused! My mind raced with what I should and should not say.

It was the cry of my heart to help my daughter begin her family after thirteen childless years of marriage, and the responsibility felt overwhelming. I did not even allow myself to feel. If this birth mother went with someone else, could we ever survive another heartbreak?

There was so much to think about with so little time. There we were, face-to-face.

This teen was the mother of a little girl who was in the care of her grandmother, and she had also terminated a previous pregnancy. What could she be thinking, feeling?

Perhaps she would feel disappointment, embarrassment, fear, and anxiety about the choices she had made and needed to make. My prayer was that she would be hopeful and relieved, but only time would tell.

In the past, I had been quite successful in sales while living in the States. I had to fight the urge to manipulate the situation and to simply trust that the Lord had everything under control, even if this birth mother went with a different family for her newborn. I wanted what God wanted. I just prayed we had the same outcome in mind.

We talked for what seemed like hours. When the employer left the room, the pregnant teen shared with me that she was scheduled for an abortion the following week. Dear Lord, the thought of this caused me to panic, and I could hardly breathe. Somehow, I simply asked her if she might still consider carrying the baby to term. She shared she was not able to care for the child financially, but she really didn't want to go through another abortion and was hopeful that someone would be willing to adopt it directly. She knew the life of babies and infants in the children's homes across the island of Jamaica and felt that was an undesirable option as they were so overcrowded already.

This young girl had gone through so much for her age. I could only imagine how full her heart was because she had to make these major decisions.

At the end of our time together, she said she wanted her mother to look at the packet and help her with the decision. In this packet, I enclosed a photo of my daughter and son-in-law, praying that putting a face with the information would help with the decision, whatever direction things went.

We arranged to meet again in six days so that the birth grandmother could come from the other side of the island to look over the packet and to meet me. This was a tremendous stretch of my faith. I had to simply wait on the Lord, allowing Him to work things out in His way, according to His plans and purposes.

For this child I prayed.

Day one, day two, day three passed; and these three days felt like a month had gone by. I had many conversations with my daughter. We shed tears together, prayed together, and even dared to dream a little. Finally, the day came when I once again headed to the employer's home, this time to meet with not only the birth mother but also her mother. Would she say that there was no way she would let her offspring be given up for adoption? Would she decide to raise a second child for her daughter? How would she feel about this child being raised so far away from his or her homeland?

Once again, I knocked on the door as my knees seemingly knocked against each other, and once again, I was ushered into the sitting room. The same anticipation arose in my heart.

Since I was a grandmother myself, I could only imagine what might be going through this woman's heart. I wanted to be compassionate and empathetic, yet I also wanted to stay as unbiased as possible so that I didn't influence anyone's feelings and thoughts.

I answered one question after another, and at the end of the hours together, I really didn't know for sure how this was all going to play out.

We ended our time together with hugs, and once again, I boarded a cab and headed to my home with the promise they would review the packet and their thoughts and let me know about their decision within a few days.

I didn't believe I could take another wait or the suspense of their decision. I wanted to call my daughter as soon as I arrived home, but what could we talk about? But I made the call, and I reviewed everything I could remember. Our emotions were all over the place.

Knowing my daughter's happiness depended on how this all went, I could hardly take the weight of the role I was playing. I have three daughters, and the other two always told Kelle they would carry a baby for her if necessary. We had all committed to doing anything we could to help them have a child. Here I was in the middle of the biggest thing they had prayed for! Lord, I could hardly breathe. I constantly had to fight the urge to over think everything, and at times I literally had to remind myself to take a deep breath.

God was merciful as always. The very next day the birth mother called me and stated they had all decided they wanted my daughter and her loving husband to adopt this newborn. I fought to stay calm—at least on the outside—and I told them how pleased I was. They could not see my tears of joy running down my cheeks or see my head in my hand lying on the table.

My heart leaped. I could barely wait to call my daughter and share the wonderful news. Could this be? Was it real?

Little did I realize this wasn't the end. It was only the beginning.

The most challenging weeks and months were ahead of us. I would soon find out that the odds of this dream coming to fruition were overwhelmingly stacked against us.

For this child I prayed.

CHAPTER 4

The Journey Begins

This young lady needed housing immediately. She had been temporarily released from her domestic housekeeper position. I did not want to see her move to the other side of the island where her family lived. First, I wanted to oversee her prenatal care since she had not even seen a doctor yet regarding this pregnancy. I also didn't want her to change her mind about the decision she had made in regard to this baby. After careful consideration, it was decided she would live with me.

Within two days of this young girl moving in with me and the other little girls in the home, we contacted a medical doctor and started going to appointments for the necessary prenatal care.

Kelle and Michael immediately set up an account with

me to cover all expenses as we went along. What a thrill! The ball was beginning to roll.

Since we had catching up to do to get the birth mother current, we proceeded with getting vitamins, making appointments, and getting the important things expectant mothers needed. The next stop was the children's clinic for an ultrasound. This expecting birth mother wasn't really interested in the gender of the baby, but the couple in Michigan was very excited to know if they were having a boy or girl. They also wanted to make sure the baby's body was developing properly. On May 3, 2006, the technician said: "Sweet baby girl face." I didn't comment because I didn't want the birth mom to get attached to the baby or second-guess her decision. That fear would stay with me until this little one left the island in the arms of Michael and Kelle. I was grateful I didn't know how that fear would affect me for the next few months. I don't know if I would have been able to take the stress.

After arriving back at our home, I went to a quiet room and phoned Kelle. I said, "You are pregnant with a baby girl," and I dropped the ultrasound in the mail to her the same day. Tears, excitement, and plans began to unfold.

Everything we did was exciting. We referred to this

baby as Kelle's daughter. We didn't mention any name or discuss her future. Mum knew what she wanted, and she was true to her word each step of the way.

One of the registration requirements to give birth at a hospital in Kingston is that someone donates blood in the birth mother's name in the event she requires some at the time of delivery. On May 16, we were off to the hospital to do just that. I had been donating blood regularly at the University of West Indies. There was always a shortage and a cry for volunteers. If I could do this for strangers, one can imagine my delight in doing it for this purpose. With the blood donated to her account, she could now register the anticipated due date as July 12.

In Jamaica, you often had to share a bed with another lady in labor, and you needed to bring with you to the hospital all your necessities, such as towels, rubber pads, pillows, etc. I took the birth mother to shop for a nightgown, robe and other items she would need, to ensure she was prepared for the big day. I kept a running ledger of expenses, and Michael and Kelle provided ample funds.

June 9 began as a very scary day. Our expecting birth mother notified me that she had not felt the baby move "since last night." I panicked. I was frustrated that I was just hearing this for the first time, and with urgency, I phoned her doctor, who directed us to immediately go to the hospital.

Dear God! We didn't make it this far to have something happen to our little baby girl, did we, Lord? Help! I needed to stay calm so that the birth mother would remain calm. This was not easy because all I could think of was my daughter back in Michigan!

The good Lord's grace fell on me, and we went right into task mode. I called the taxi. The other children in the home were sent off to school with their lunches. I lined up someone to be there for them after school in the event I was not. Mum was nervous and grateful I was accompanying her since she had given birth to her previous baby all alone.

The elevators at the hospital were out of order. *Are you serious!* There I was, carrying all the belongings necessary for this event and helping a young pregnant girl up to the fourth floor via the stairs while she was doing her best to carry herself and keep her balance in this state. We came up to other mothers in the same situation on the steps. Some of them were behind us. I thought, *Just make it to the top, sweetheart.* We arrived at 10:30 a.m., and she had still not felt any fetal movement. I didn't want her to climb stairs, but it was the only way for her to get where she needed to be.

The fact that she felt no movement was far more of a concern to us than it appeared to be for the staff. They simply said, "Someone will be here to see her in the next several hours." The minute one becomes aggressive or short with staff, their defenses go up, and you get nowhere. After that, you aren't given any information, and they might make you leave completely. I couldn't risk that happening, so I became their friend. I should not have been allowed inside the ward, but when I told them I was "experienced and would be glad to give them a hand," they welcomed me. I wasn't necessarily experienced, but I believed I could do something to help. Plus, I knew they were severely understaffed. By 3:30 p.m., doctors saw the birth mother and detected a heartbeat. Thank You, God! Soon after that pelvic check, labor began, and it went as planned. At 7:23 p.m., this little blessing came forth. They told me her birth weight was "3.1". I was caught off guard! I realized this baby had made her appearance nearly five weeks early. Her weight was not okay! After calming down, they assured me that the measurement was in kilograms, (I assumed it was pounds) and she weighed six pounds four ounces.

Oh, hallelujah! This was quite a good size for a baby girl from a petite birth mother, especially since she was born a month premature. Truly, the birth of a baby is a miracle.

The hospital insisted I leave once the baby was born, and to be honest, I could hardly wait to get home and give Kelle and Michael the marvelous update! Their baby girl was here, and they didn't even have to wait until July 12, 2009.

Tears flowed. We started making plans. We both chatted so much we likely missed some of what the other was saying. Our emotions ran high. Our hearts welled up with excitement, and the once buried dream began to come to life again.

For this child I prayed.

CHAPTER 5

Not without My Daughter

Chloe was born on a Friday night, and by Saturday night, I was looking forward to bringing her home. I had been shopping on King Street in downtown Kingston to get the final supplies, and so I felt quite prepared. On Saturday afternoon, Mum had a fever. They didn't allow the newborns to have a bottle in the hospital, and with a fever, breastfeeding was a concern.

For this child I prayed.

Thankfully, by Sunday morning, Mum was feeling fine. She phoned me and said her mother was coming from the other side of the island. She asked if I would be willing to meet her mother in downtown Kingston and bring her to the hospital. She wanted to see the baby before they were discharged. Instantly, I felt sick. Natural instincts had me fearful that the birth grandmother would want to keep this baby.

I readily agreed, but my heart was pounding! I feared that if she saw this adorable little one, her heart would be so captured she would not be able to let go. However, since it was Mum's request, I complied. I didn't want to do anything to upset Mum and give her second thoughts. I met the birth grandmother at a little restaurant and treated her to a meal since she had been on the road for quite some time, and then we proceeded to the hospital. Since I had been up to see Mum every visiting hour possible, the staff recognized me as her mother, so I was the only one able to go up to the nursery. Down the four flights of stairs, carrying pillows, blanket, towels, nursery items, Mum's personal items, and the little papoose, and stabilizing the birth mother, we emerged out the front door to a welcoming bench and to a waiting birth grandmother.

Looking back, I can only imagine the sight of the three of us with all of those belongings, but at the time it was anything but amusing.

With my heart racing and pounding so hard, I was afraid those nearby would hear it. I handed the newborn over to her grandmother. I felt like I was going to throw up. *Please, Lord, don't let her fall in love with this little darling!* But I had to allow the grandmother to hold her. I would have wanted the same opportunity if the tables were turned, and if she was going to have a change of heart, I would rather she have it now than months down the road when things were progressing and Kelle and Michael were opening their hearts to this little angel.

The Bible says in Hebrews 11:6, "Without faith, it is impossible to please God." I knew He would be pleased that day. Faith is all I had, and all my faith was in Him.

Suddenly, the grandmother asked me to take the baby. She said it was time to go. Because her comment was unexpected and so abrupt, I wanted to know how she was feeling. So I asked. She assured me this was the right decision. She wouldn't have encouraged it if she didn't know me personally. They knew this little one was already loved and would get the opportunity of a lifetime growing up in the United States. The birth grandmother was not going to be a threat, and she would encourage and stand behind her daughter in the decision. *Okay, I can relax,* I thought. *At least a little.*

I proceeded to call two taxis, one for Mum and the grandmother and one for the baby and me. When the first cab arrived, the driver was not familiar with the address where the other two needed to go, so I asked him to take the baby and me and to get directions for the second driver. The cab was parked rather far away. I could not bring the items to the cab and leave the baby with mum, and I couldn't put the baby in the cab and come back for the items. I could hardly carry everything and the baby, but I found a way. There piled high was a pillow, blankets, baby items, a diaper bag, and a six-pound baby girl. It felt like a balancing act, but off we went. I looked out the tinted windows of the cab, and I was so afraid I would see the birth mother running after the cab. I told the driver to "get going." I have thought about this often, and I imagine that was how Sally Field felt in the movie *Not without My Daughter*.

Whether Mum and the grandmother discussed this at all, I will never know. Leaving this newborn's blood relatives behind was something I only considered for a few minutes. We were progressing as Mum had chosen, and I knew this little one was going to have an amazing journey ahead of her.

Her story began then.

I was fifty-eight years old when I brought this angel

home from the hospital forty-eight hours after her birth. It had been years and years since I had been around a newborn, and there was a lot of experimenting to get everything right. Up to this point, this beautiful newborn was simply referenced as the baby. Now that we have her in the safety of my home, we will now call her Chloe. Kelle and Michael gave me the privilege of naming this little girl they prayed would one day be able to come home with them. I named her Chloe- meaning vibrant and one who searches, and Kelle and Michael gave her the middle name of Isabelle which means consecrated to God and discerning spirit. What an honor to name this baby. My heart still wells with joy at this fact.

The very first night we were home, I became alarmed. Chloe hadn't had a messy diaper, and her breathing sounded rattling. I called Dr. John at the children's clinic at 11:00 p.m., and he assured me all was well. I just needed to give Chloe some glucose water. To make sure she was all right, I fell asleep praying for her and holding hands with this little angel through the slats of her crib. This began a routine of holding hands every night for some time during the night, and it persisted even years later. Chloe still like the comfort and closeness of one-on-one with her mom for fifteen minutes each evening prior to going to her beautiful room for the night. Sorry, Mommy and Daddy. That's my fault.

Holding hands

For this child I prayed.

CHAPTER 6

Bureaucracy Maze

I looked forward to having a few weeks to get used to the new routine of a baby and very little sleep, but that was not the case. Much had to be done to get on course to begin the long and tedious process to adopt this little one. In Jamaica, the mothers do not *register* their newborns with the government at the hospital when they give birth, which would make perfect sense to me. Rather these young ladies who gave birth just days prior need to find their way back to this very same place. I met Mum there without her new birth daughter. We had a live-in helper we called Auntie who was more than happy to take care of this little bundle of joy, and I was not about to have Mum begin bonding with this newborn.

When Mum was asked by the registration people the

name of the birth father, I had hoped she would say she didn't know (which was quite unfair of me) because then we wouldn't have to get surrender paperwork from him when the time came, but she listed him by name. She listed the name of the newborn as she had named her, but in my heart, I had quite a different image of this precious little one.

After the registration had transpired, we went our respective ways once again. I cared deeply for this young teen, and I was truly concerned about how she was doing. We stayed in touch but never discussed any details about the newborn. She had chosen a name for this baby, and when we mentioned her, I used the name she'd selected. I don't believe she knew the name we chose for this little one, and that seemed best—at least for the time. I simply referenced her as the baby.

When I read this and reminisce, it sounds cold to me; however, I was trying to maintain a distance for everyone's benefit.

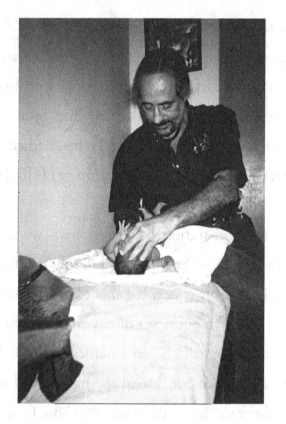

Dr. John praying over Chloe

Two days later, baby Chloe had her first doctor's appointment. Friends of mine owned and operated a children's clinic in Kingston, and Uncle John was Chloe's doctor. He handled her as if she were his own child or grandchild. I believe at one point when he was checking out her heartbeat, I even saw his eyes close. I truly sensed he was praying over this little one. We will always be grateful for the excellent care Chloe received there. I was also grateful that they allowed me to register her with the name Chloe and her soon-to-be adoptive parents' last name. It all seemed surreal and promising. We thought it would all be finished soon.

The schedule kept filling up with necessary appointments. I was getting more and more tired, and all I wanted was to stay home and enjoy this newborn and the other girls living with me. There were three older girls in the home, little girls who had stories of their own, but they were all very loving and happy to welcome baby Chloe. Of course, Chloe was going to be spoiled with so much love in the family and everyone wanting to hold her and play with her. These were such delightful days and wonderful memories.

Next, I had to get eight copies of the birth certificate at the registrar general's office. We had to use the name the birth mother gave for the baby, and that seemed disappointing. It was for the best that this office did not know the baby was going to be adopted; especially to patents who lived outside of the country. Things may have been handled differently if this were the case. Chloe would need to take up residence in one of the many overpopulated and understaffed children's homes in Jamaica. She could be sent anywhere across the island. I was a licensed foster home, so it only made sense that she stay in my care. We could not risk losing touch with this baby, even though the birth parents had granted guardianship to Michael and Kelle, the "system" might decide otherwise. We may never have seen Chloe again. Little did we realize that more than a year would pass before we could even hope for this placement to occur. At least she was in our care.

When the birth certificates arrived in the mail, I made my way to a lawyer to find out what the necessary steps were to start this legal matter. She came highly recommended by the pastor of the local church I was affiliated with. I will call her "Auntie Shirley," and this dear saint began our time together with prayer. I couldn't think of a better way to begin or anyone I would rather have worked with at this stressful time. After an hour or so of discussion, Auntie Shirley assured me that we now had things in order and that I could easily proceed on my own. I said, "Okay, thank you so much." But my heart said, "No! Don't abandon me!" It probably wasn't quite as serious as abandonment, but since I had no idea what I was doing or what I needed to do, I surely wanted to stay connected to this woman.

Six weeks after giving birth, the birth mother met with the children's agency. The birth parents needed to be legally identified. Appointments like this took organization and expense along with the cooperation of both birth parents. I sent money via Western Union for their travel expenses, told them when and where I needed them, met them at the bus depot, bought them dinner, and escorted them from one place to another.

It is the custom in Jamaica to do everything in their power to convince the birth mother to keep her child, which is admirable. While Mum was in with the agency representative, I was in the adjoining room, pacing quite anxiously. Would Mum be swayed by these seemingly pushy workers who were only doing their jobs? Would Mum's original plans of surrendering her newborn stay intact? Would she have regrets or second thoughts?

For this child I prayed.

CHAPTER 7

Calm during Danger

In the following days, the normal developments with a newborn took place. We began to find a routine. She had regular wellness checkups and made substantial progress. Chloe even found her voice. She noticed it one morning and startled herself. She would be quiet and then make noises, which would startle again. It was such a delight to watch, but then as a grandma, I thought every development was marvelous.

August 19 came. This is one of the biggest dates I can remember up to that point. Kelle came to meet her Chloe in person and to spend two weeks with her. (I guess she came to visit me too, but only a little). Kelle looked at Chloe from head to toe and observed everything that made her unique and special. She cried, held her, rambled a thousand words, and took a multitude of photos. She needed to call Daddy to tell him everything, and there were even more tears. It was wonderful. We didn't have a speakerphone, but I could hear Michael share Kelle's absolute joy.

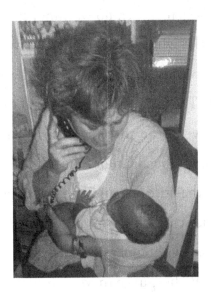

On the phone with Daddy

There were lots of people for Mommy to meet. She met the lawyer we were so blessed to work with and also Dr. Sheree, Mum's doctor. She met Uncle John at the children's clinic. She had an appointment with the children's agency and the lady from my church who gave me the name and number of the original domestic helper's employer.

What began as a wonderful family night with Mommy, Chloe, and the three other little girls living with me became a frightening experience. We were in the family room at the back of the home, laughing and watching TV, and the older girls were putting on a little show for Kelle and Chloe. Suddenly, with no warning, there was gunfire right outside the windows. Fortunately, we had louvered windows so no one could see in, but the horrific noise was alarming. The little girls were used to the routine and headed directly up the three steps into a room with no windows. Kelle grabbed Chloe, and while crawling on the floor, she held the little one underneath her body to protect the baby while scrambling to safety. Since our backyard was surrounded with concrete walls that were eight feet high, we knew the gunman was inside the perimeter. Living in Jamaica, one always keeps their doors locked, so we simply turned out the lights and stayed in the center of the house for more than an hour. This routine had become all too familiar.

The little girls needed to shower and get to bed, so I escorted them down the hallway and remained outside the bathroom door while they showered. By this time, a couple of hours had passed. There were no further signs of danger sensed, so they each went to bed.

Unfortunately, a second event took place a week later. This time there was gunfire in our front yard, and there were glass windows in the room we were in. Kelle tossed Chloe into the corner of the bed away from glass. She had experienced about all the dangerous and threatening activity she could take, and she found solace in calling Michael.

Mommy brought down a shirt for Chloe that said, "It's all about me," and it surely was. With the drama we had just experienced, Kelle became convinced they needed to get Chloe home to Michigan as soon as possible.

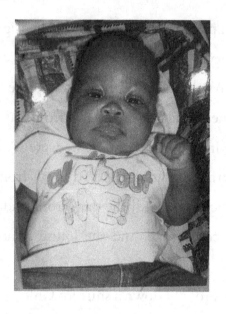

It's all about me

We went to dinner at a restaurant, and Mommy and I played cards there; however, we mainly talked about Chloe, the future, and our feelings. We were so excited and yet apprehensive. Little did we know the wait had only just begun.

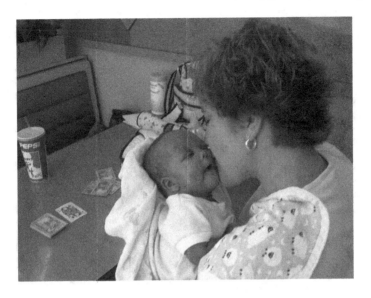

Taking a break from cards to love on the baby girl

August 30 came all too soon. Mommy's time was over, and she had to get back to Michigan. It was horrible taking her to the airport. Kelle was so concerned for everyone's safety because of what had recently transpired. She just held on to Chloe and didn't want to let go.

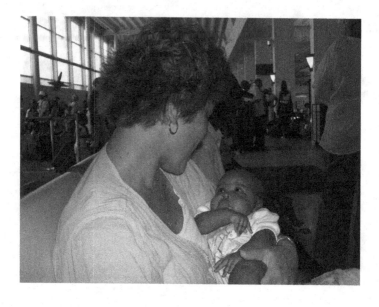

Heartbreaking departure

The following months were filled with routine living and normal development for Chloe. She gained weight in a normal fashion, crawled at six months, pulled herself up at seven months, stood by herself at eight months, got her first tooth at nine months, got her second tooth at ten months, and sipped from a straw at eleven months. I documented every milestone with photos, and it seemed I went to the photo lab and post office at least once a week with pictures to send to Michigan. That was before our family had Facebook or texting, and there were way too many photos to send via email. I was excited to do this and could only imagine Kelle and Michael's excitement to check their mailbox and receive each envelope.

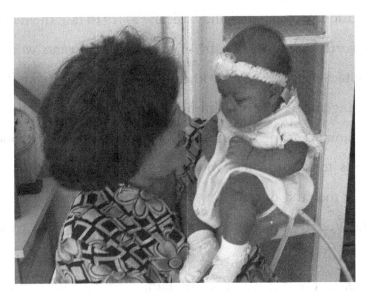

Nana and Chloe

Throughout the course of Chloe's development, I would often put her on my shoulders. We would make a game of it. I would lean from side to side, and I would say with a chuckle, "Don't fall." She would giggle, and sitting on my shoulders soon became her favorite place to be. We were close, and I was still able to make phone calls or do computer work and correspondence. Until I became too old and she became too big, she would often be content to hang out just that way.

On February 7, the birth parents were summoned to court. The purpose was to explain exactly what their decisions would entail and basically to try to talk them out of surrendering their baby once again. The agents would contact me because they knew I would have to make the arrangements to get them here from wherever they were in Jamaica at the time. I kept supplying them with phone cards to ensure they would keep communication open with me, and once again, I would forward them money via Western Union, meet them at the bus terminal, treat them to a meal, and escort them to the appointments and back to the bus terminal. In Jamaica, they didn't travel in luxurious buses with padded seats. These were coaster vans with too many passengers and a driver who was too anxious to get from point A to point B. In his view, the faster he went, the more trips he could make in a day. People never felt assured they were safe, and each time they would reach their destination safely, everyone breathed a sigh of relief.

The days and weeks following were nerve-racking. Each time I met with the birth parents, I felt pressured to say and do everything right to keep them on board with their choice. I didn't want to patronize them, and I didn't want to minimize the severity and permanency of their decision.

Following every encounter of this type, I would go back to my home, try to jot down things to remember, and always follow up with a phone call to Kelle in Michigan. There were so many critical stages to this endeavor that it seemed there was never an opportunity to just take a deep breath and relax.

I basically had no one to share what I was feeling with. If I had been as honest with Kelle as I wanted to be, she would surely have been a wreck. This was a lot to deal with alone, but I had the dream that this was all more than worth it because my daughter and her sweet husband would soon have a child of their own. Each day was intense for me, but the emotions Mike and Kelle were experiencing thousands of miles away were unimaginable.

The next time Kelle and Chloe would see each other was June of the following year for Chloe's first birthday. Kelle boarded a jet in Grand Rapids, Michigan, and headed to Kingston, Jamaica, to visit her soon-to-be daughter. The plans abruptly changed. Because of a late arrival in Miami, Kelle missed the last jet out to Kingston. The next one would not be available until the next afternoon. She could catch a flight to Montego Bay, which was on the other side of the island and still reach Kingston the day she had hoped. We agreed to those arrangements, and I called a taxi to bring Chloe and me to meet her all the way in Montego Bay. There was no way she would be able to sit in an airport so far away for another day, knowing that Chloe missed her too. What a day! There we were in Montego-Bay, with hours of traveling to get back to Kingston, but Kelle and her little angel just cuddled together in the back seat and took a much-needed nap. She took photos of every movement the little one was making, and then Kelle went to the phone the minute we arrived at my place in Kingston.

Kelle and I ordered a birthday cake that was quite expensive but well worth it for such a memorable occasion. However, when we picked it up, it was a disaster. All we could do was laugh, and when we got home, we had to basically pull the frosting around to even make it presentable. Chloe opened her gifts, and the other little girls in the home giggled right along with her as she discovered each one. They were such wonderful big sisters, and we were sure to let them know how special they were as well. The photos will always be part of Chloe's life, and one day we will tell her all about these amazing little ones she was so blessed to have in her life.

Humorous flop

One very special gift Michael and Kelle got Chloe was a preemie Cabbage Patch doll with the birth date of July 12, which ironically was Chloe's original due date. They didn't know the doll's birth date until after they opened the box.

We made a point of doing special things while Kelle was in Jamaica. We swam in a kiddy pool in my front yard. Now that was a sight to behold. We also went to Rockford Mineral and to Lime Cay, which to this day are two of my favorite spots in the world.

Chilling out

All too soon Kelle had to go back to Michigan. It was even harder this time. When she left, I quietly smuggled her nightgown out of her luggage. I wanted her delicate scent to stay at the home for Chloe to have, and from that day until Michael and Kelle came back to Kingston, I never washed that nightgown. Chloe snuggled with it every night and naptime. This little one missed Kelle, and this would enable Kelle to remain in Chloe's world in her absence. We had no idea when the next meeting would take place. Only time would tell.

I kept many appointments with different workers of the children's agency. It seemed that they didn't always know what the other was doing, but that could have just been my frustration in wanting things to move along quicker.

As we got further along, the worker I was assigned to shared with me that on Mondays, they would determine what cases would be heard in family court on Thursday of that week. We didn't hear anything July 2, but we held out hope that we would hear on July 9 that our case would be scheduled for that Thursday. We did not get the call on the 9th, nor the 10th. Noon on Wednesday, the 11th. came and went. What a disappointment since that Thursday would have been July 12, the date on the birth certificate for Chloe's preemie doll and the birth mother's original due date. Kelle and I talked on Wednesday afternoon and expressed the disappointment we both felt. To be honest, now we didn't know what to hope for. I wanted so badly to cry, to talk to someone, but this was a very personal walk I had to go through alone. Adopting a baby out of Jamaica was unheard of, and very few people locally would have understood my position or empathize with me.

At 5:17 p.m. on Wednesday, July 11, an hour after children's agency was closed, my phone rang. It was the agency worker asking if I would be able to be in court the following morning at 9:00 a.m. They had a cancelation.

We didn't have an answering machine, and I just thanked the Lord I was home to receive that call. "Of course I can make it," my heart cried, but I simply said, "Sure, I look forward to it."

Immediately, I phoned Kelle and Michael, who nearly screamed when they heard that we had gotten our court date the very next morning! This hearing would see if the court would indeed grant custody to them and if the birth parents would totally surrender their child. Did I simply miss this pertinent information, or did the good Lord not want the new mommy and daddy to be overly anxious?

Little did I realize that while I was preparing to go to court that following morning, Michael and Kelle were heading to the airport in Michigan to fly to Jamaica. They thought they would finally be able to take their baby home to Michigan. I guess they believed that would take place immediately. I am sure they were just overwhelmed with emotion that things had reached this point ... and on the very day we prayed for.

On July 12 at 8:50 a.m., I met with the children's agency representative at family court in downtown Kingston. We were advised by the Adoption Agency Board that the judge assigned to our case was very tough and would be a challenge for us. He would do everything in his power to convince the birth parents to keep their child. The purpose of today's hearing was to permanently sever the parents' rights to the baby and thus make her a ward of the state, which is a requirement of the Immigration Department of the United States.

Family court

I put a blanket over Chloe, a pacifier in her mouth, and a hat that was way too big for her to cover her head. (Fortunately, it was chilly, and this made some sense.) I was just sure if the birth parents got a good look at this precious child that they would have second thoughts. I also didn't want them to see her darling face etched in their minds. That could be haunting. I knew we would be seeing them any moment, and I just could not let them see her.

Hat used to disguise Chloe

My stomach was rumbling. I was shaking, and I wasn't even sure that I was aware of everything going on. I went to the left of the courtroom where I was escorted. The birth parents were directly to my right. I kept Chloe facing away from them.

I kept saying a silent prayer, "Lord, open my mouth. Lord, close my mouth." I did not know what this judge would be looking for. I couldn't tell what the birth parents were feeling and thinking. I had to believe that the judge would agree to terminate the birth parents' custody, and I also hoped that he would allow this infant to leave her native country so that we could raise her thousands of miles away!

For this child I prayed.

CHAPTER 8

So Near and Yet So Far

There we were, at family court—a Jamaican child, birth parents, a judge who strongly favored children remaining with their original families, and a white woman speaking for an American couple seeking custody of this Jamaican child and wanting to take her from her homeland. The odds were not in our favor.

It all came down to this. The judge questioned the birth father rather aggressively first, challenging him to basically change his mind about surrendering his daughter. He responded, "No, mon, me nah need no more pickney." When he questioned the birth mother, she said that she cared about the child but could not give her what she would require for a good future—food, shelter, and schooling.

She added that her extended family supported her in her decision.

The judge looked at me. I had this beautiful child hidden from everyone, covered with a blanket and hat. You would have thought we were in frigid weather. I pointed to the air conditioner above me as if to say that was why the child was covered. He smiled, and I believe he totally understood that I was hiding her.

His next comments were beautiful words to my ears and heart. "The parental rights of the parents are hereby severed, and this infant is now a ward of the state." Then some words rolled off my tongue without me thinking. I believe it was the Spirit of God speaking over the whole situation. "God bless you, Your Honor, and God bless this couple as well. I believe God used this couple and their situation for His plans and purposes. This child is *no* accident."

The birth parents were dismissed.

Once the birth parents left the room, the judge continued by saying, "I can clearly see that this infant is not merely surviving but thriving in the care of this home. It is further determined that all requirements have been met by the prospective parents. I hereby declare full parental custody to Michael and Kelle."

I had to fight dropping to my knees to praise God or sitting and bawling. I maintained my composure (don't ask me how) and thanked the judge for his very fine work on behalf of this child, my grandchild.

The children's agency representative working with me said she would prefer I stayed right at the courthouse until I had the proper paperwork. Had we left, things could have gotten misplaced, and we might have had to endure another time-consuming delay. By 4:00 p.m., we left with my little granddaughter in my arms and the paperwork clinched tightly in my fist.

It would have been great if Mike and Kelle could have packed up Chloe when they arrived in Kingston and turned right around and taken her home to Michigan. Bureaucracy never works so smoothly. While the children's agency and the court had approved of the process going forward, the American embassy would have the final word.

On one of the many trips that Michael and Kelle took Chloe to the American embassy, one of the employees noted how sensible Chloe was. She exuded joy and a sweet and charming character, and she seemed to develop quickly for her age. The worker asked Mike and Kelle what children's home she was in, and they replied, "Beacon of Hope," a foster home on Snowden in Kingston. This was the name I had given the home I was overseeing. They supplied the requested phone number of Beacon of Hope, and I received a phone call the following day from a representative from the American embassy stating that they would like to come and see this place themselves. I felt anxious. What if they asked me questions I had not wanted to answer? What if they wanted to know if I knew the prospective adoptive parents? Would it make a difference if they knew that Kelle was my daughter?

They came, and Chloe was such a sweetheart that she captivated their attention. They simply enjoyed their visit and wished me well in this home for little girls, and then they were on their way.

One appointment at the embassy for Mike and Kelle followed another. Each time they went to the embassy, it was as though the sea of hundreds of people waiting in line to be seen would swing wide open for them, and they were escorted right to the front. What could have meant long hours of waiting in the hot sun or the rain with no overhead canopy was really only a minimal wait time. This was truly seen as God's favor.

At one appointment with the American embassy, the officer asked Michael if he had ever met the birth parents. He answered truthfully by saying no. Had they asked Kelle, she would have had to honestly answer yes. Kelle had met with the birth mother on more than one occasion, and these two became much like sisters. They both had a common desire for this child to have a wonderful future. We did not know if or how that information would affect the process. Would it have held up the progress or stopped it altogether? While Mike and Kelle were simply a loving American couple desiring a family and the chance to give a little one the love and opportunities they could, the officer may have been suspicious they were buying this little girl for their own gain or other purposes. The selling and trafficking of children was a disgusting but genuine concern for the heads of departments. God intervened once again.

However, the American embassy brought to our attention that they could not see where the birth father had signed one necessary document. *Are you serious?* I thought. *Are they just looking for things to hold this up?* I contacted the birth father, who was on the north side of the island, and sent him money to travel, telling him I needed him at the children's agency in the morning. I never knew if they were going to cooperate, and every time something like this transpired, there was reason to raise concern. The following morning the birth father phoned me from the bus depot and told me that he had made it to Kingston. I boarded a cab, went to get him, and delivered him to the necessary office. I couldn't risk that he would not show up where he was needed, so I escorted him there. Kelle took a separate cab to the children's agency. Michael and Chloe were already at the American embassy, awaiting Kelle's arrival with the signed paperwork to take care of this business.

When it came time for the notary to sign the birth father's document, she asked him for identification to validate his signature. He had not taken it. Of course, ID was required. The notary didn't know him and could not attest to the validity of his identity. He was hours from Ocho Rios, where his passport was, and it would be impossible for him to take another day off work to take care of this. Dear God, *help!*

For this child I prayed.

I called my contact at the children's agency, and without hesitation, he told the notary, "If Pennie says this is who he is, that is who he is. Her word is good." I didn't know if he said as much because he knew me so well from all my interaction with the children's homes, my hours and hours of work at many government functions, my living at the children's homes during hurricanes, or something else, but I was thankful nonetheless. The notary signed the papers, and I was dismissed. I thanked the birth father and gave him return money so that he could get back to the north side of the island and have some dinner too. I proceeded to run as fast as I could down the corridors to the elevator. I went down nine flights of stairs as fast as I could and pushed the signed document into Kelle's hand. She rushed into downtown King Street and hailed a cab, and once again, she made her way to the embassy.

One more hurdle crossed.

On July 30 at the embassy, Kelle and Michael were told it would likely be another three to four weeks before things would be in place for them to leave the island with their daughter. It had already been weeks since they had gotten the paperwork from the court. Mike and Kelle needed to get back to their jobs in Michigan, and their hearts had taken about all the waiting and suspense they could handle.

It would have been easy to become discouraged, impatient, and even defensive. However, that would have been the very worst thing we could have done at that point. It would likely have closed the doors too tight to ever open them again.

We called our prayer partners in the States, and together we all prayed, "Your Kingdom come, Lord, and Your will be done." It was our turn to surrender this child.

For this child I prayed.

CHAPTER 9

Shocking Turnaround

Without expecting to hear anything for a while, Kelle, Michael, and I, along with the other young girls living in my home, took to seeing some attractions around Kingston for the next couple of days, and we played a whole lot of Nickel-Nickel, my favorite card game to this day.

En route to Lime Cay Island

On Thursday, August 2, I ventured out to the grocery store to stock up once again. Kelle gave me their debit card to get whatever we needed. I walked around rather aimlessly for forty-five minutes, not feeling prompted to buy meat, bread, eggs, milk, or any of the things I had set out for. I returned an hour or so later, and the only things in the grocery bag was small bags of chips, food bars, and bottled water. I had no idea what I was up to, but I learned long ago to follow my instincts. I took myself by surprise here, but within hours, it would all make sense.

At 10:00 a.m. the following morning, August 3, the American embassy phoned me. They asked if I would be able to get ahold of Mike and Kelle. They didn't know Kelle was my daughter and standing a mere eight feet from me at the time. I simply told them, "Yes, how can I help?"

Just four days after the American embassy told us it would be a minimum of three to four weeks before we would be able to move forward, they were now telling me that the baby was missing one shot required for traveling. They added that if we could get her that shot right away and be to the embassy by 1:00 p.m., they could leave today for the United States. I calmly said I would inform them and assured the embassy that they would be there by 1:00

p.m.. Upon hanging up the phone, we began dancing, screaming, and crying!

We called my cab to take us to the closest hospital, where there were forty to fifty people in line for the same office. *Dear God, how will we ever get there in time?*

We went to each person in that line and asked if we could move up after we explained the situation. While many of them fussed about us, asking who we thought we were, they ushered us forward, sensing something amazing was going on. When we got to the front of the line and were next to being seen, we were told we needed to pay before Chloe could have the injection. I took the invoice and ran down the hospital corridor to accounting. I was back to the office with the receipt before they had Chloe's sleeve rolled up.

As quickly as we made our appearance at this hospital, we disappeared. Kelle, Michael, and Chloe ran out to the parking lot and got into the waiting cab, and they were off to the American embassy. I took another cab and went back to the house.

The reality of what was transpiring was overwhelming. I wanted to make phone calls, but there was much to do to get this little family out of town. I quickly packed all of their things, including Chloe's. I also packed the chips, bottled water, and food bars I had purchased the night before. God knew what we would need for groceries. I love it when He leads that way! My heart was so torn. I loved my life with Chloe in it. I knew, however, that it had been temporary, and now it was the honor of Kelle and Michael to take over as Chloe's official mom and dad.

While I finished the last load of their laundry and put the fresh clothes in their luggage, they drove up. They were elated, dancing together. We all cried, and Michael began making phone calls to the airlines. The next possible flight to the United States left the following morning out of Montego Bay. They could have flown at noon out of Kingston, but leaving immediately for Montego Bay would be the safest thing to do. This way, if anyone tried to contact them for any last-minute changes or questions, we could truthfully say we didn't know how to get ahold of them. While I prepared their last meal in Kingston, they made calls to Michael's mother and sister in Georgia, his dad and other sister in Michigan, and Kelle's siblings also in Michigan. Everyone was thrilled. The day had finally come for this family to begin their marvelous journey together as a mommy, daddy, and child.

A kind gentleman at the children's agency made hotel reservations for Michael and Kelle in Montego Bay, and he was also instrumental in getting Chloe's passport in a matter of hours, which would ordinarily have taken days. This was another example of God's favor. I have heard it said that karma is real. Through the years I have personally contributed many hours and resources to the orphans and needy little ones of Jamaica. Now good was coming to my family, and Jamaica was giving back in a very tangible way. Galatians 6:7 says, "Do not be deceived, God cannot be mocked, a man reaps what he sows." That has been proven over and over. It always pays to try to be the answer to another's need, to use our gifts and means to be a blessing, and to let God be the one who rewards. His plans are greater than anything we could hope for or imagine. Ephesians 3:20a says, "Now to Him who is able to do immeasurably more than all we ask or imagine."

As my taxi driver drove up, the baby seat installed in the back seat of his van, we began packing the things that were going back with them. This angelic baby girl, who had lived in my home for fourteen months and had experienced all of her *firsts* there, was moving thousands of miles away. My heart could hardly take the thought of my life without her. I had been consumed with Chloe and everything about her from before her birth until now. I would need to find a new normal once again. There was only one reason I could rejoice at this stage, and that was the fact that my beautiful daughter and her wonderful husband would have their very own child, which they had been dreaming of for more than a dozen years.

Just two months later, my father became ill. I didn't need to rush home to try to mend anything or say any unspoken words. We had our marvelous times together while he was well. He passed away, and I was called to Michigan for his memorial service. As a blessing, I had to go to the very town where Michael and Kelle had taken their baby girl. They met me at the airport, and that was a perfect delight. My other daughters and their beautiful families were there too. My heart was so blessed. Little Chloe remembered me immediately and ran right past everyone else to get to me. When I scooped her up, she pointed to my shoulders. She wanted to sit high on Grammy's neck. "Of course, you can, baby girl. That is your spot," I said. She knew I was still in her life, and I had the comfort of knowing she would never forget me.

This child was born for greatness. She is the first child

for Michael and Kelle, and Chloe has also had incredible, prophetic words spoken over her. We will leave those to unfold in God's way and in God's timing.

For this child I prayed ... and do pray.

Chloe on Nana's shoulders

Afterword

To close, I want to quote a portion of a book I am reading titled *Telling Secrets* by Frederick Buechner, one of my favorite authors. Referring to writing his life story, he says,

> Maybe nothing is more important than that we keep track, you and I of these stories of who we are and where we have come from and the people we have met along the way because it is precisely through these stories in all their particularity, as I have long believed and often said, that God makes himself know to each of us most powerfully and personally. If this is true, it means that to lose track of our stories is to be profoundly impoverished not only humanly, but also spiritually.

It's official in Michigan!

Open house for Chloe in Michigan

Printed in the United States
By Bookmasters